Mohammadreza Rast

IELTS Writing Updates 2

Mohammadreza Rast

IELTS Writing Updates 2

IELTS Writing Task 2 Topics, Instructions, Tips, Vocabularies, Grammars, Collocations, Phrases and Band 9 Samples

Noor Publishing

Imprint
Any brand names and product names mentioned in this book are subject to trademark, brand or patent protection and are trademarks or registered trademarks of their respective holders. The use of brand names, product names, common names, trade names, product descriptions etc. even without a particular marking in this work is in no way to be construed to mean that such names may be regarded as unrestricted in respect of trademark and brand protection legislation and could thus be used by anyone.

Cover image: www.ingimage.com

Publisher:
Noor Publishing
is a trademark of
Dodo Books Indian Ocean Ltd., member of the OmniScriptum S.R.L Publishing group
str. A.Russo 15, of. 61, Chisinau-2068, Republic of Moldova Europe
Printed at: see last page
ISBN: 978-620-2-34424-1

Copyright © Mohammadreza Rast
Copyright © 2021 Dodo Books Indian Ocean Ltd., member of the OmniScriptum S.R.L Publishing group

IELTS Writing Updates 2

IELTS Writing Task 2 Topics, Instructions, Tips, Vocabularies, Grammars, Collocations, Phrases and Band 9 Samples

Compiled by :

Mohammadreza Rast

Introduction

The second part of the writing test in IELTS is **Writing Task 2** , where a point of view, argument or problem is presented and you are asked to write an essay . Your written style must be a formal one, at least 250 words in length and you should consider to complete your essay in 40 minutes. Everything that is needed to aim a band +9 mark is gathered and compiled in this book. They are topics, instructions, tips, vocabularies, grammars, collocations, phrases and band 9 samples.

Mohammadreza Rast

February, 2020

Instructions

When helping students prepare for the IELTS test, one of the biggest fears is how to do well in IELTS Writing Task 2. It doesn't matter if you're new to IELTS or if you've failed the exam before – I've broken everything down into a simple process that anyone can use to improve their bands.

How to Get a Band 9 in IELTS Writing Task 2

1. Understand the question

You must understand the question *before* you attempt to answer it. This way, you'll know exactly what the examiner is looking for. One of the biggest mistakes students make is not answering the question fully, which stops them from getting a score higher than a Band 5.

To analyze the question, you must first identify the question type, then identify the keywords in the question and finally identify the instructions words. This will help you understand exactly what the examiner wants you to do with the question.

2. Plan your answer

The students who get the highest marks in Writing Task 2 always plan their answers for up to 10 minutes. Planning helps you organize your ideas and structure your essay before you write it, saving your time and helping you produce a clear and coherent essay.

3. Write an introduction

The introduction should tell the examiner what the rest of the essay is about and also answer the question directly. This tells the examiner that you know what you are doing straight away and helps you write your main body paragraphs.

4. Write the main body paragraphs

This is where you give the examiner more detail. You do this by stating your main points and supporting these with explanations and relevant examples.

5. Write a conclusion

In your conclusion, you should provide a summary of what you already said in the rest of your essay.

Ways to Improve your Score in IELTS Writing

Many people know they need to improve their writing skills, but they have no idea *how* to do it. Here are 4 ways you can boost your score in Writing Task 2:

1. Understand the exam.

You must first understand what IELTS Writing Task 2 is, what you are expected to do and how to give the examiners what they want. This is the first stage and one that is often overlooked.

There are a huge number of online resources, often with conflicting and poor-quality information, so finding a reliable source of information is key.

2. Identify your weak areas.

If your car breaks down, you would try and identify which part caused the problem. If you get sick, your doctor will run tests to find out the exact cause of your symptoms.

IELTS Writing Task 2 is exactly the same. We must first identify WHY you are not getting the score you need before we can help you improve.

However, be very careful! You wouldn't ask the average man on the street for medical advice, so make sure you find someone who actually knows what they are doing and have the expertise to help you with this.

3. Fix the problems.

Now that we know what the problems are, we must fix them.

If your grammar needs work, fix those issues. If your vocabulary is lacking, work on fixing this issue.

Just like a good doctor will be able to help you fix a medical problem, a good IELTS teacher will be able to help you fix your specific issues.

4. Practice and get feedback.

Practice alone will not help you. It is an essential part of your preparation, but you must also get feedback on your work if you are really going to improve. You wouldn't try to teach yourself how to drive without an instructor, would you?

Find someone who will give you accurate and helpful feedback on your work. Otherwise, you will not be able to move to the last stage.

Structures

One thing I would like to warn you about structures is that they are not a magic wand that will help you automatically get a higher score. They WILL help you, but please realize that they are just a small part of your overall score.

These structures provide a sentence-by-sentence template for all the main Task 2 question types, making your job much easier on exam day.

Skills

No matter how good your English is, you still need to learn IELTS writing skills before you take the Writing Task 2 test. These helpful guides will take you through each of these skills step-by-step:

Plan an Essay

Making a good plan actually saves you time when you write your essay. This guide will show you how to plan and write a clear essay every time.

Think of Relevant Ideas

Write a Complex Sentence

Complex sentences help you boost your score for grammar. They are actually very simple to write and are not complex at all.

Paraphrase

Paraphrasing is one of the essential IELTS skills for all parts of the IELTS test. You should paraphrase the question in the very first sentence of your essay to help boost your vocabulary score in Writing Task 2.

Write a Supporting Paragraph

Supporting paragraphs are the main body paragraphs and are the meat in the sandwich. This is where you provide the detail the examiner is looking for in the form of explanations and examples.

Thesis Statement

A thesis statement tells the examiner your opinion. Many IELTS Writing Task 2 questions specifically ask for your opinion and if you don't write it clearly you have not answered the question properly.

How many words should I write?

Around 250 words. Exactly 250 words or over 250 words.

Understand and Analyse Any Question

A critical part of answering any question. to break down any Task 2 question and identify the keywords, micro-keywords and instruction words to help you answer the question effectively.

How to Write a Great Introduction

The introduction is the first thing the examiner reads and it is, therefore, essential that we give them a good first impression.

How to Write a Conclusion

A good conclusion should be a summary of your main points. The conclusion is the last thing the examiner reads and if you can write a good one you will leave them with a very good impression.

Using Examples

Each of your supporting paragraphs should have a specific example that supports and illustrates your main point. This is an essential skill to learn if you want to get one of the higher band scores.

Cohesive Devices

Cohesive devices (sometimes called linking words) are one of the most misunderstood and misused elements of writing. Therefore, you must learn how to use them and when to use them.

The Danger of Synonyms

While synonyms are very important, they can also really reduce your mark if used incorrectly.

How to Impromve Your Band

Learn how to go from a Band 6 to a Band 8 in IELTS Writing. Those are :

Paragraphing and Editing

To make your writing as clear and as easy to read as possible. It will also give you advice on whether to use a pen or pencil.

Common Topics

Knowing the common topics can help you prepare for the test more efficiently. Here are the 10 most common topics over the last few years. Studying hard is great, but don't forget to study smart.

Practice

Here are some lessons that I have used when teaching students about IELTS Writing Task 2. I have changed them so that you can easily learn. They are combined with the skills above; they contain all the information you need.

- **Agree or Disagree (Opinion) Questions**

In this section, we look at how to tackle an 'agree or disagree' question. Many people worry about whether to take one side of the other or if to discuss both sides. Additionally, people also worry about how to deal with 'To what extent' question types. We allay all of these fears in these questions.

- **Discussion Essay Questions**

'Discuss both views' questions often cause confusion because you are asked to do many things in one essay. As such, it is very important to remember that the question is asking you to discuss BOTH views AND give YOUR opinion.

- **Problem and Solution Essay Questions**

These questions are much easier than you think. You probably discuss problems and solutions in your day-to-day life all the time. Keep it simple.

- **Advantages and Disadvantages Questions**

There are a couple of different types of advantages and disadvantages questions.

Sample Answers

It's very important that you have some good examples so that you can compare your writing and see if you are on the right track.

Grammar and Vocabulary

Grammar is one of the four things you will be marked on in the Writing Task 2 test. Finding out what your common grammar mistakes are and then fixing them is a very powerful way to boost your score in this area.

- **Grammar Mistakes**

For most IELTS students, the problem is not grammar in general. In fact, it is usually just 1-2 problem areas. Therefore, when you fix these main weaknesses, you'll be able to improve your grammar and your writing score dramatically.

- **Using Personal Pronouns**

IELTS Writing Task 2 Essential Information

1. You must write an essay in response to a question.

2. It is important that you write 250 words or more.

3. Task 2 is worth 2/3 of your total mark on the Writing test.

4. You should spend around 40 minutes on this part of the test.

5. General Training and Academic are essentially the same for Task 2. However, they are different for Task 1.

6. There are certain types of questions that you will be asked, for example, opinion, discussion etc. See below for more detail on these.

7. You will be assessed in four areas:

    1. Task Achievement (25%)

    2. Coherence and Cohesion (25%)

    3. Lexical Resource (25%)

    4. Grammatical Range and Accuracy (25%)

+250 Writing Task 2 Topics

February / March 2021

Some people say that all popular TV entertainment programmes should aim to educate viewers about important social issues. To what extent do you agree or disagree with this statement?

Some people believe the purpose of education should be helping the individual to become useful for society, while others believe it should help individuals to achieve their ambitions. Discuss both sides and give your opinion.

Many people believe that a person's culture is defined by their country of origin, while othersbelieve that it has only minor influence. Discuss both these views and give your opinion.

More and more people are finding it increasingly important to wear fashionable clothes. Is this attitude to wearing clothes a positive development or negative?

The movement of people from villages to cities for work can cause serious problems in both places. What are the serious problems associated with this? What measures can be taken to solve these problems?

In the world of the internet, people write product reviews of products and services. Do you think this is a positive or negative development?

Some people prefer to buy local products while others prefer international products. To what extent do you agree or disagree?

Some believe that more action should be taken to prevent crime, while others feel that crime is being tackled effectively now. Discuss both sides and give your own opinion.

Some people say it is more important to plant trees in the open spaces in towns and cities than to build more housing. To what extant do you agree or disagree?

Some scientists think that computers will soon become more intelligent than humans.To what extent do you agree or disagree with this statement?

Some people think that dangerous extreme sports such as rock climbing and sky-diving should be banned. To what extent do you agree or disagree with this view?

Young people are often influenced by their peers. Do the advantages of peer pressure outweigh the disadvantages ?

Some people believe that nowadays too much money is being spent on weddings and birthdays. Why do you think it is happening? What can be done to improve the situation?

In many countries, the legal driving age is 18 years old. Some people believe it is the right age to learn how to drive a car, whereas others say that the minimum age should be. Discuss both views and give your opinion.

Some people think that instead of preventing climate change, we need to find a way to live with it. To what extent do you agree or disagree?

January 2021

Some people feel that the effects of advertising are positive for individuals and businesses, while others think they are negative. Discuss both sides and give your own opinion.

Some people say that TV advertisements are helpful for viewers, while others disagree. What is your opinion?

Some people think the spread of multinational companies and globalization produce positive outcomes for everyone. Do you agree or disagree with this statement?

In some countries, there are fewer young people who listen to or play classical music these days. Why is this? Should young people be encouraged to play or perform classical music?

Directors of large organizations earn much higher salaries than ordinary employees do. Some people think it is necessary, but others are of the opinion that it is unfair. Discuss both views and give your own opinions.

Prison is the common way in most countries try to solve the problem of crime. However, a more effective solution is to provide people with a better education. Do you agree or disagree?

Some think that climate change reforms will negatively affect business. Others feel they are an opportunity for businesses. Discuss both sides and give your own opinion.

Some people argue that holding sporting events is beneficial to a country's development. However, other people hold the opposite opinion. Discuss both views and give your own opinion.

The first man to walk on the moon claimed it was a step forward for mankind. However, it has made little difference in most people's lives. To what extent do you agree or disagree?

Some people think that good teamwork makes a company successful, others think that good leadership is the reason behind the success of a company. Discuss both sides and give your opinion.

October/November 2020

Nowadays more and more people want to get things done instantly. Why is it? Do you think it is a positive or negative development?

Some people think that it is a waste of time for high school students to study literature, such as novels and poems. To what extent do you agree or disagree?

In some countries the elderly are highly valued and respected, while in others youth is more highly valued. Discuss both sides and give your own opinion.

The personal information of many individuals is held by large internet companies and organisations. Do you think the advantages of this outweigh the disadvantages?

Some people believe that handwriting is no longer useful in the modern world and should not be taught in schools. To what extent do you agree or disagree?

Some believe that advances in technology are increasing the gap between rich and poor while others think the opposite is happening. Discuss both sides and give your own opinion.

More and more people are finding it increasingly important to wear fashionable clothes. Is this attitude to wearing clothes a positive development or negative?

Some people believe that smart phones are destroying social interaction today. To what extent do you agree or disagree?

Some people believe that governments should ban dangerous sports. Others claim that they should have freedom to choose their favourite activities. Discuss both views and present your opinion.

Nowadays employment options are changing and employees cannot rely on having the same job and working conditions throughout their life. What are some possible causes? Suggest some ways to plan for the future under these circumstances.

August 2020

Many companies sponsor sports as a way of advertising themselves. Some people think this is good for the world of sport, while others think it is negative. Discuss both views and give your own opinion.

Governments in many countries have recently introduced special taxes on foods and beverages with high levels of sugar. Some think these taxes are a good idea while others disagree. Discuss both views and give your opinion.

Many people think technological devices such as smart phones, tablets and mobile phones bring more disadvantages than advantages. To what extent do you agree or disagree?

It is better for children if the whole family including aunts, uncles and grandparents are involved in a child's upbringing, rather than just their parents. To what extent do you agree or disagree?

Most people prefer shopping in supermarkets nowadays. How does this affect the local shops? What are the positive and negative impacts of this development?

In many countries, fast food is becoming cheaper and more widely available. Do the disadvantages of this outweigh the advantages?

The government should lower the budget on the arts in order to allocate more money to education.To what extent do you agree?

Many people argue that eating junk food has led to an unhealthy lifestyle. This problem has become more common among young people these days. Do you agree or disagree that junk food is the cause of the issue?

Some people think that in order to produce a happy society, it is necessary to ensure that there is only a small difference between the earnings of the richest and poorest. To what extent do you agree or disagree?

The manufacturing and use of cars damages the environment but their popularity is increasing.Why is this happening? How could this be controlled?

March 2020

Some people think that young people should go to university to further their education while others think they should be encouraged to work as car mechanics or builders etc.to serve society. Discuss both views and give your own opinion.

Some people believe that to give opportunities to the new generation companies should encourage high level employees who are older than 55 to retire. Do you agree or disagree?

Nowadays celebrities earn more money than politicians. What are the reasons for this? Is it a positive or negative development?

Many people believe that countries should produce food for the whole population and import as little food as possible. To what extent do you agree or disagree?

Some people think that it is necessary to travel abroad to learn about other countries, but others think that it is not necessary to travel abroad because all the information can be seen on TV and the internet. Discuss both views and give your own opinion.

Why are some people who leave school early more successful compared with those who complete their studies. Provide reasons why they are more successful and what are the requirements for success?

Countries with long average working hours are economically more successful than those countries which do not work long hours. To what extent do you agree or disagree?

Many students around the world don't choose science subjects at university. Give the reasons for this and describe the impact on the community?

It is better for young people to get advice from old people than young ones. Do you agree or disagree?

Some people think that music plays an important role in society. Others think it is simply a form of entertainment. Discuss both sides and give your opinion.

Some people think that job satisfaction is more important than job security. Others think that people cannot expect to enjoy a job and that having a permanent job is more important. Discuss both views and give your opinion.

Some people say that technologies such as mobile phones are disrupting social interaction. Do you agree or disagree?

Some people think history has little or nothing to offer, while others say the study of the past helps us understand the present. Write on both views and give your opinion, citing examples from your experience

Some people think that zoos are cruel and all the zoos should be closed. However, others think that zoos are useful to protect rare animals. Discuss both views and give your own opinion.

Some people think that the best way to stay fit is to join a gym/health club while others think doing everyday activities such as walking and climbing stairs is sufficient. Discuss both views and give your opinion.

January 2020

Nowadays online shopping is extremely popular. Discuss the impact of it on the environment and on people who lost their jobs because of it.

Nowadays celebrities earn more money than politicians. What are the reasons for this? Is it a positive or negative development?

Many people think that every individual is responsible for their happiness, but some people believe there are other external factors that influence us. Discuss both views and give your opinion.

It is too expensive to look after and repair old buildings. This money should be spent on building modern buildings instead. To what extent do you agree or disagree with this opinion?

Scientific research should be the responsibility of governments rather than commercial organizations. Do you agree or disagree with this statement?

Some people believe that women should be treated as equal to men when applying for a job with police or the military. Others think women are less suitable for this kind of job. Discuss both views and give your opinion.

Some people prefer to work in the same type of job throughout their lifetime while others like to change the type of job they do. Discuss both views and give your opinion.

Some people think that it is fine for professional sportsmen and sportswomen to misbehave on or off the field, as long as they are playing well. Do you agree or disagree with this statement?

People are becoming too dependent on the Internet and phone. Is it a positive or negative development?

Some people suggest that it is better for children to be brought up by the whole family including uncles, aunts and grandparents, rather than just the parents. Do you agree or disagree with this statement? Give your opinion and examples.

Some people think that the government should increase tax on unhealthy food to encourage people to start eating healthy. Do you agree or disagree?

Nowadays, people are spending more time away from their homes because they spend longer in their workplace. Discuss the advantages and disadvantages.

Nowadays a few people take their family with them abroad whenever they go on a business trip. What are the advantages and disadvantages for them and for their family?

Many parents complain about violence promoted to their children through video games, TV programs and other media. Why is it happening? What can be the solution for it?

October 2019

Nowadays most people are not as fit and active, as they were in the past. What are the main causes of this situation? Suggest some possible solutions.

Nowadays, international tourism is the biggest industry in the world. Unfortunately, it creates tension rather than understanding between people from different cultures. To what extent do you agree or disagree with this opinion?

Fossil fuels (e.g. coals, oil and gas) are the main source of energy for most countries. However, alternative sources of energy (e.g. wind and solar) have been encouraged for use by some countries. To what extent is this a positive or negative development?

Nowadays media should include more good news in their publications. Do you agree or disagree with this statement? Give reasons for your answer and include any relevant examples from your own knowledge or experience.

Fossil fuels are the main source of energy around the world. However, people are being encouraged to use alternative energy sources such as wind energy, solar energy and so on. Do you think this is a positive or negative development? Why?

Some people believe that elderly employees are more useful to a company, while others believe that young employees are better. Discuss both views and give your own opinion.

The number of older people is increasing. Some people think that this will cause problems in their countries, others believe this group is important to society. Discuss both views and give your own opinion.

Some think that teenagers should follow older people's rules. Others thinks that it is natural for them to challenge what older people say. Discuss both views and give your opinion.

Television Sporting shows such as the Olympics motivatethe youth who do not like to exercise much. Do you agree or disagree? Include relevant examples in your answer and provide your own opinion.

Nowadays many people want to buy famous brands of clothes, cars and other items. What are the reasons for this? Do you think it is a positive or a negative development?

More people live alone today than they did in the past. Do you think this is a positive or negative development? Give your opinion and relevant examples to support your view.

Some people believe that price is the only consideration when buying something. Do you agree or disagree with this statement? Give your opinion and include relevant examples.

Some people believe that educational success depends on good teachers, while others believe that students' attitudes are important. Discuss both views and give your opinion.

People in the current generation are not fit and active. This will cause health problems in the future. What could be the reasons for the inactivity and suggest solutions for this issue.

Parents, usually mothers, stay at home to look after their families. People believe that for this they should receive a salary from the government. Do you agree or disagree and why?

Some people think that they can go to the gym to remain fit, while others think that there are other better ways to do this. Discuss both views along with your opinion.

Some people say companies should require all employees to wear uniforms at work. Others think it is unnecessary. Discuss both views and give your own opinion.

Because of modern technology, some people believe that it is no longer necessary for people to learn handwriting skills, but others believe that handwriting is still an important skill. Discuss both views and give your opinion based on your experience.

Nowadays many people work from home. Some think it is beneficial, while others think it may distract the family routine. What is your opinion?

It is necessary for parents to attend a parenting training course to bring their children up. Do you agree or disagree?

Nowadays people work too hard. What is the reason for this? What should employers do to prevent employees from over working?

Nowadays people get married and have children after the age of 30. Is it a positive or negative development?

Today, some young people say that their mobile phones are the most important thing they own. Do you think that the popularity of mobile phones is a good or bad thing?

Nowadays, people believe that governments should invest tax-payer's money in healthcare, others believe that money should be use in other areas. Discuss both points of view and give your opinion.

September 2019

Adults do less exercise nowadays. Some think that people can be encouraged to live healthy lives through sporting events such as the Olympics or the World Cup. Others think that there are better ways to encourage adults for exercise. Discuss both views and state your opinion.

Modern cultures around the world have become similar when compared to the past. What are the reasons? Is it a positive or negative development?

People are using a lot of online language translation apps. Are there more advantages than disadvantages to such services.

Demand for food is increasing worldwide. What is the cause of this? What measures can the international community take to meet this demand?

Many companies sponsor sports as a way of advertising themselves. Some people think that this is a good thing, while others think that it has disadvantages. Discuss both views and give your own opinion.

Some people believe that to be successful at a sport you need natural ability and others think that hard work and practice can make you successful. Discuss both views and give your opinion?

Nowadays, adults do little exercise. Some people believe that the best way to address this issue is by covering great sports events such as the Olympics n television. Others think that it is more beneficial to take other measures. What is your opinion?

These days some people spend a lot of money on tickets to go to sporting or cultural events. Do you think this is a positive or negative development?

Some people believe that technology has made man more social and others think that it has made him less social. Discuss both views and give your opinion?

Experts say older people were happier and healthier in the past because they did more exercise and spent more time with family and friends, whereas many now suffer from loneliness and health problems. What are the causes of this and what are some solutions?

August 2019

Some people believe that to be successful at a sport you need a natural ability and others think that hard work and practice can make you successful. Discuss both views and give your opinion?

Some people believe that there will be a reduction in air travel in the future. Do you think that this trend is a positive or negative development?

Some people believe that technology has made man more sociable and others think that it has made us less sociable. Discuss both views and give your opinion?

At the present time, the population of some countries includes a relatively large number of young adults, compared with the number of older people. Do you think that the advantages of this outweigh the disadvantages?

Some people believe that it is important to give gifts to friends and family to show that we care about them. Others think that there are better ways to show that we care. Discuss both views and give your opinion.

Today much of the food people eat gets transported from farms that are thousands of miles away. Some people believe it would be better for the environment and the economy if people only consumed food produced by local farmers. Would the advantages of this outweigh the disadvantages?

With internet improvements, people can share views or opinions on certain goods or services that they have purchased. Is this a good or a bad thing? Discuss both views and give your opinion.

The qualities and skills that a person requires to become successful in today's world cannot be learned at a university or any other academic institution. To what extent do you agree or disagree?

Shopping has become a new favourite pastime for younger generation. Why is this the case? Should we encourage them to develop other hobbies too?

Courses and general online study have recently become very popular. However, some people still prefer to attend classes in person. Discuss both views and give your own opinion.

Some people think that prison sentences should not be used to deal with criminals. Education and skills training should be used instead. To what extent do you agree or disagree?

It is often said that it is not necessary to have a tertiary education to become a successful businessman. To what extent to you agree or disagree with this statement? Give your opinion and relevant examples.

Today it is common practice for many business meetings and business training to take place online. Do the advantages of this new development outweigh the disadvantages?

Nowadays, internet and television have given ordinary people a chance to become famous. Is this a positive or negative development?

Some people from poor and rural backgrounds find it difficult to get a university education. Universities should make it easier for such groups to enrol. To what extent do you agree or disagree?

Some people think that it is the responsibility of governments to take care of the environment, while others believe that it is the responsibility of the citizens. Discuss both views and give your opinion.

Many people believe that family has a greater influence on a child's life and development than other factors, such as friends, TV, music and so on. Do you agree or disagree with this statement?

Science can now offer people a life expectancy of close to one hundred years or even more. Some people view it in a positive light, but others believe it creates some problems. Discuss both views and give your own opinion.

These days, many people prefer ready to eat food outside of their home rather than homemade food. Do you think this has more advantages or disadvantages?

Certain personal qualities cannot be achieved through university studies. Do you agree or disagree with this statement? Give your opinion and relevant examples.

In some countries the quality of life in larger cities is declining. Why do you think this is happening? What measures can be taken to stop it?

June 2019

Shopping is now one of the most popular forms of leisure activity in many countries for young adults. What do you think is the reason for this? Is this a positive or negative development?

In many countries, people are living in a "throwaway society" where things are used for a short time and thrown away. What are the causes of this and what problems does it lead to?

In some countries, people follow the latest fashion and hairstyles. In your opinion, what is influencing this? Do you think this is a positive or a negative development?

In some countries, children under 16 years old are not allowed to leave school by law and get full-time work. Is this a good or bad thing? Discuss your opinion.

Nowadays, people have adopted an unhealthy lifestyle. Why do think this is? How could this problem be solved?

Some young people are leaving the countryside to live in cities and towns, leaving only old people in the countryside. Why do think this is? Do you think this is a positive or a negative development?

In many countries, people have more health problems because they choose to live an unhealthy lifestyle. What do you think are the reasons for this and how can it be solved? Give relevant examples from your experience.

Countries with a long average working time are more economically successful than those countries which do not have a long working time. To what extent do you agree or disagree?

Nowadays, people of all ages from certain parts of the world spend most time at home rather than going outdoors. Discuss the reasons, is this negative or positive development?

With the development of technology and science, some people believe that there is no great value of artists such as musicians and painters. What are the things artists can do but the scientist cannot? Should art be encouraged more?

January 2019

While recruiting a new employee, the employer should pay more attention to their personal qualities, rather than qualifications and experience. To what extent do you agree or disagree? Give your opinion and include relevant examples.

Money should be spent on creating new public buildings such as museums or town halls rather than renovating the existing ones. To what extent do you agree or disagree?

All the people in a company should be treated equally and provided with the same number of holidays in a year or people doing different jobs enjoy different amount of holiday time. To what extent do you agree or disagree?

Some people say that a person's success is as a result of the way he has been brought up by his parents. Do you agree or disagree?

Public celebrations (such as national days, festivals etc) are held in most countries. These are often quite expensive and some people say that governments should spend money on more useful things. Do you agree or disagree?

Some people prefer to buy local products while others prefer international products. To what extent do you agree or disagree?

Some people say that children given pocket money every week will have lesser money problems when they become adults. Do you agree or disagree?

The global demand for oil and gas is increasing. Some people believe that we should therefore encourage the exploitation of remote areas. Do the advantages of this outweigh the disadvantages?

Today, many big cities in the world are increasing in size. What are the problems associated with it? What are the solution to these problems?

Some young people are leaving countryside to live in cities or towns, it leaves only old people in countryside. What are the problems of this issue? What can be done to solve this problem?

Many people believe that learning a foreign language is a very difficult task. What are the most difficult things about learning a foreign language? What is the best way to overcome them? Explain and include your personal experience or knowledge of these problems.

Some people think high-end technology can prevent and cut down the rate of committing crime. Do you agree or disagree?

Some people feel that courses can make anyone a teacher, while others feel an excellent teacher cannot be made by pursuing a course. Discuss both views and give your opinion.

Some people think that high salary is important when choosing a company to work for, while others think that good working atmosphere is more important. Discuss both views and give your opinion.

Some people encourage young children to leave their parents house as soon as they become adults while other say children should stay at their parents house as long as possible. Discuss both the views and give your opinion.

Many countries thought that children have to do homework in their free time while other say children should do more outdoor activity. To what extent do you agree or disagree?

Some people say that art subjects such as music, drama and creative writing are an essential part of education, and every school should include them in its syllabus. Do you agree or disagree with this statement? Give your opinion and examples from your own experience.

Nowadays in many countries women have full time jobs. Therefore, it is logical to share household tasks evenly between men and women. To what extent do you agree or disagree with this statement?

Some people think that public health within a country can be improved by government making laws regarding nutritious food. Others, however, think that health is a matter of personal choice and responsibility. Discuss both views and give your opinion.

Many people believe that learning a foreign language is a very difficult task. What are the most difficult things about learning a foreign language? What is the best way to overcome them? Explain and include your personal experience or knowledge of these problems.

Some people believe that construction of new public buildings such as museums, town halls and sporting facilities is more important than renovation of the existing ones, while others disagree. Discuss both views and give your own opinion.

Nowadays the crime rate is increasing, especially among teenagers. What are the reasons behind it? How can we reverse this trend? What punishment methods should be used, in your opinion?

Nowadays online education has become popular as more institutes and companies are offering courses online. However, many people prefer the traditional, classroom training or study. Discuss the advantages and disadvantages of both methods.

Some people believe that the government should take care of old people and provide financial support after they retire. Others say individuals should save during their working years to fund their own retirement. What is your opinion? Give reasons for your answer and include examples from your own experience.

In some cultures old people are valued more, while in other cultures youth is considered more valuable. Discuss both views and give your opinion.

Some people say that art subjects such as music, drama and creative writing are an essential part of education, and every school should include them in its syllabus. Do you agree or disagree with this statement? Give your opinion and examples from your own experience.

Nowadays people waste a lot of food that was bought from shops and restaurants. Why do you think people waste food? What can be done to reduce the amount of food they throw away?

December 2018

In today's times internet is making it easy to study online from home. Some prefer online courses to study and they think it is better. Others prefer classroom education. Discuss both views and share your opinion.

Successful companies use advertising to make more sales. What can make an advertisement very effective? Do you think this is a bad thing or a good thing for the society?

Science will soon make people live up to 100 or even 200 years. Some believe this is a good thing while others disagree. Discuss both views and give your own opinion.

Some people believe that after hundred years life will be easier for most of people, while the others are unsure. What is your opinion?

Some people think it is important to spend a lot of money on a wedding celebration, while others disagree. Discuss both views and give your opinion.

Some people think that giving gifts and presents to friends and family is important to show them that we care. Others think that there are more important ways. Discuss both and give your opinion.

The media is increasing interest in famous people who have ordinary backgrounds. Why do you think people are interested in the lives of famous people? Do you think this is a good thing?

Some people prefer activities and lifestyle in hot climates while others prefer activities and lifestyle in cold climate. Discuss both views and give your opinion.

Online education and training is becoming increasingly popular in the business world. Do the advantages of this development outweigh the disadvantages?

More and more parents are allowing their children to play on computers and tablets as they think that children should learn technology skills. Do the advantages of this development outweigh the disadvantages?

People are living in a 'throwaway society', using things for a short time and then throwing them away. What are the causes of this? What problems does it lead to?

Nowadays children mostly spend time playing computer games rather than sports. What are the reasons for this? Is it a positive or a negative development?

Scientists agree that many people eat too much junk food and it is damaging their health. Some people think that this problem can be solved by educating people, while others believe that education will not work. Discuss both views and give your own opinion.

Many people believe that TV news and media in general have a detrimental effect on our life. Do you agree or disagree with this statement? Give your own opinion, including relevant examples.

Many famous athletes advertise different products. What are the advantages and disadvantages of it?

Nowadays people try to balance their work with other things in life, but only some could actually achieve it so far. What are the reasons for that? How can we solve this problem?

Some people say that online study is the most effective and convenient way to learn. Others believe that online study will never be as effective as learning at school, in person. Discuss both views and give your own opinion.

Children and teenagers are committing more and more crimes in many countries. Why is this happening? How can we stop or at least reduce youth crime?

Some people prefer cold weather conditions, while others don't. Discuss both views and give your own opinion.

Some people think subjects taught in school are a waste of time, while others disagree and believe that this type of education is useful for students. Discuss both views and give your own opinion.

November 2018

Some people think that the only way to relax is rest or sleep, while others say people need to do exercise or sport to relax. Discuss both view points and give your own opinion.

Some parents and teachers think that children's behaviour should be strictly controlled. While some think that children should be free to behave. Discuss both the views and give your opinion.

In many countries day by day rubbish (garbage) is increasing. Why is it happening? What can be done?

Some people see shopping as a leisure activity mostly for young adults, while others disagree. Do you think this has a positive or negative effect on economic development? Give your opinion and include relevant examples.

Shopping has become a favorite pastime among young people. What do you think it is like that? Do you think they must be encouraged to do other things rather than shopping?

Some people think that the main factors influencing a child's development these days are things such as television, friends, and music. Others believe that the family still remains more important. Discuss both views and give your opinion.

Food travels thousands of miles from producers to consumers. Some people think that it would be better for the environment and economy if people only ate the local food produced by farmers. To what extent do you agree or disagree?

Some people argue that the fittest, strongest individuals and teams can achieve the greatest success in sports. But other people think that success is as much related to mental attitude. Discuss both views and give your opinion.

Some people become famous when they are at a young age. Do you think this is positive or negative?

Some people believe it is important to give gifts and presents to friends and family to show that we care about them. Others think that there are better ways to show affection to them. Discuss both the views and give your own opinion.

Many people believe that spending a lot of money on weddings is fine, while others completely disagree. Discuss both views and give your own opinion and examples.

Many people believe the government should spend money on faster public transport. Others think that money should be spent on different aspects of public transportation, such as cost reduction and environment conservation. Discuss both views and give your own opinion.

Some people believe that manufacturers should be responsible for reducing the large amounts of packaging they use. Others say consumers should avoid buying heavily packaged items. Discuss both views and state your opinion. Give reasons for your answer and include examples from your experience.

Some people think that family has the most important influence on children's development, while others believe that factors such as TV, friends, music and books have a more significant impact. Discuss both views and give your opinion.

October 2018

Today, most people get married and give birth in their thirties rather than when they are younger. Is this a positive or negative development?

Shops should give preference in selling local food rather than imported food. Do you agree or disagree?

Growing population is a big problem in developing countries. Should the government provide new homes in the cities or countryside?

Some people think that the media (newspapers) have the right to publish details of people's private lives, while others think it should be controlled. Discuss both views.

Some people think that activities during the free-time should be planned while others disagree. Discuss both sides and include examples and relevant data from your own experience.

In some countries an increasing number of people are suffering from health problems as a result of eating too much fast food. It is therefore necessary for governments to impose a higher tax on this kind of food? To what extent do you agree or disagree with this opinion? You should use your own ideas, knowledge and experience and support your arguments with examples and relevant evidence.

Today more people are overweight than ever before. What in your opinion are the primary causes of this? What measures can be taken to overcome this epidemic?

In most parts of the world people are living longer. What are the possible causes of this situation? Is this a negative or positive development?

Today, the internet and TV have created that chance for ordinary people to become famous. Is it a positive or negative development?

Nowadays food has become easier to prepare. Has this change improved the way people live? Give reasons for your answer using your own ideas and experience.

Nowadays many people believe that children should be taught history in schools, however, others argue that children should learn subjects that are more helpful for modern everyday life. Discuss both views and give your own opinion.

Some parents believe that a child should not waste time by reading entertainment books, instead they should spend time to read educational books only. What is your opinion about this?

Some people think that young children need to attend nursery before primary school. While others believe young children can spend all day at home. Discuss both views and give your opinion.

Some people believe school children should be given multiple short vacations while others believe they should get one long vacation. Give advantages of both and your point of view.

Some people think that the advantages of advertising sports products through famous sports players outweigh the disadvantages. To what extent do you agree or disagree?

In our society, there is far more attention on men's sport than women's sport. What are the reasons for this? Do you think that this is positive or negative development?

It has been said that reading for pleasure is better in developing imagination and language skills than watching TV. To what extent do you agree or disagree?

Advertisements are influencing us in a negative way. To what extent do you agree or disagree?

School teachers are more responsible for the social and intellectual development of students than parents. To what extent do you agree or disagree?

Some people spend a lot of money for their wedding ceremonies. However, others feel like it is unnecessary to spend a lot. Discuss both view points and give your own opinion.

Since traveling abroad became relatively inexpensive, more countries opened their doors for foreign tourists. Is it a positive or negative trend? Give your opinion and include relevant examples.

Many countries consider eighteen year olds to be adults, while other countries don't. What do you think about it? Give your opinion and some relevant examples based on your own experience.

September 2018

Some people think that the only way to judge someone's success in business is by the amount of money they make. Is this a true indicator of the success of a business and in what other ways could success in a business be measured?

The restoration of old buildings in major cities around the world costs enormous amounts of money. This money would be better spent on providing new housing and road development. To what extent do you agree or disagree with this opinion?

Employers should give their workers at least one month holiday a year as it makes them to do better at their job. To what extent do you agree or disagree?

Some people believe the Olympic Games doesn't belong to the 21st century anymore. To what extent do you agree or disagree?

Some parents believe that reading books for entertainment is a waste of time for children and they think that their children should only read serious educational books. What is your opinion?

Some people think that an advertising on TV is useless and others disagree. Discuss both sides and give your opinion.

Some people think money is the best gift to give it to youngsters, while others disagree. Discuss both the views and give your opinion.

For school children, their teachers have more influence on their intelligence and social development than their parents. To what extent do you agree or disagree?

In the modern world it is possible to shop, work and communicate with people via the internet and live without any face-to-face contact with others. Is it a positive or negative development in your opinion? To what extent do you support this development?

Many university students live with their families, while others live away from home because their universities are in different places. What are the advantages and disadvantages of both situations?

In the modern world it is no longer necessary to use animals for food, clothing or medicine. To what extent do you agree or disagree? Give reasons for your answer and include examples from your own experience.

Some businesses observe that new employees who just graduated from a college or university seem to lack interpersonal skills needed for communication with their colleagues. What could be the reason for this? What solutions can help address this problem?

Some people believe that we should start giving formal education to students at a much earlier age, while others think we should wait until the age of 7. To what extent do you agree or disagree with this statement? Discuss and give reasons for your answer.

Nowadays in many countries young people leave rural areas to study or work in cities. What are the reasons for this? Do the benefits of this outweigh the disadvantages?

Some parents believe that reading entertainment books is a waste of time. In their opinion, children should only read serious, educational books. Do you agree or disagree? Give reasons for your answer and include relevant examples from your own experience.

Nowadays there is a growing trend of private car ownership. Do the advantages outweigh the disadvantages or environmental problems associated with this?

Some people believe that companies should pay for damage they cause to the environment, while others say that the government should be responsible for such expenses. Do you agree or disagree? Give reasons for your answer and include examples from your experience.

Nowadays there are many medical surveys of treatments to reduce health problems. Who should conduct them, governments, individuals or private companies, in your opinion? Give reasons for your answer and include relevant examples from your experience.

The international community must act immediately to ensure that all countries reduce their consumption of fossil fuels such as gas, oil and coal. To what extent do you agree or disagree with this statement? Give your own opinion.

August 2018

For school children, their teachers have more influence on their intelligence and social development than their parents. To what extent do you agree or disagree?

Many people believe that it is a good idea to have a dress code at workplaces. Do you agree or disagree with this statement? Give your opinion and examples from your own experience.

Some think that private companies should pay for pollution clean up, while others say it should be a government's responsibility. Discuss, and state your own opinion.

Many people think that more having more money will make them happier. How important is money to happiness?

Many people believe that the use of new technology improves the lives of employees. Others think it is a disadvantage for them. Discuss both views and give your own opinion.

Some people say that sport is very important for a nation's development, while others believe that sport is no more than a leisure time activity. Discuss both views and give your own opinion.

Some people think that children should start school sooner while others believe they should not start it before the age of seven. Discuss both views and give your own opinion.

Some people argue that competitive sports are good for bringing together different people and cultures. Others argue that these sports can cause problems and increase conflicts between nations. Discuss both points of view and give your own opinion.

In some countries, it is illegal for employers to reject job applications on the basis of age criteria. Is it a positive or negative development? Give reasons for your answer and include examples from your own experience.

Many young people regularly change their jobs over the years. What are the reasons for this? Do the advantages outweigh the disadvantages?

Some people think that new technologies benefit the life of workers whereas some deny the statement. Discuss both sides and give your opinion.

Scientists agree that many people are eating too much junk food and it is damaging to their health. Some people think that these problems can be solved by educating people to eat less junk food. Other people believe that education will not work.
Discuss both opinions and give your own opinion.

Some people think that companies and private individuals should pay to clean up the pollution that they produce, not the government. To what extent do you agree or disagree?

As more and more students enter universities, academic qualifications are becoming devalued. To get ahead in many professions, more than one degree is now required and in future, it is likely that people will take a number of degree courses before even starting work. This is an undesirable situation. To what extent do you agree or disagree?

Many people are involved in sports when they are young but stop once they are adults. Why do many adults stop doing physical exercise? What can be done about this problem?

Some people think that it is a good idea for all employees to wear a uniform at work. To what extent do you agree or disagree?

Some people think that new technology always improves the lives of workers. Other people believe that it results in disadvantages for workers. Discuss both opinions and give your own opinion.

Some people think that international competitive sports such as football bring conflict between people of different age groups and nationalities. Others think the sport is helping reach understanding between people and nations. Discuss both views and give your opinion.

Some people think that only staff who worked in the company for a long time should be promoted to higher positions. What is your opinion on this? Give reasons and relevant examples for your answer.

Some people think it's a good idea to wear a uniform at work. Do you agree or disagree? Give reasons for your answer with relevant examples from knowledge or experience.

Some people think it is more important to spend time in developing a successful career while others think it is more important to spend time with friends and family. Discuss both sides and give your opinion.

There is less social contact between young and old. What are the reasons? What measures can be taken?

July 2018

Do you agree with the following statement: home schooling protects students from a number of challenges faced by non-home-schooled children?

Does distant learning make it easier for students to balance their everyday lives?

Learning in one's native tongue yields better school scores than learning in a medium language.Do you agree or disagree? Argue your point of view.

Should there be a variety of learning methodologies implemented within the school learning curriculum?

July 2018

Some believe that modern technology has made people less socially active, while others disagree. Discuss both views and give your own opinion.

The best way to reduce crime among young people is to teach parents good parenting skills. To what extent do you agree or disagree with this statement? Give your own opinion and examples.

Some psychologists think that the best way to overcome stress of everyday life is to spend a portion of the day doing absolutely nothing. To what extent do you agree or disagree?

There is a trend of increasing amounts of consumer goods, which leads to environmental problems. What are the reasons for this trend? Give your own opinion and solutions.

The difference in age between parents and their children has increased compared to the past. Do you think advantages of this trend outweigh the disadvantages?

Scientists have been warning for many years already that in order to protect the environment people should use less energy. However, most people do not change their ways of living. What is causing this behaviour? How can people be encouraged to change?

Some people think that children should go to kindergarten before attending primary school, while others believe that is better for children to stay all day with their families. Discuss both views and give your own opinion.

Some people believe that trade and cultural relationships between the countries is a positive development, while others disagree. Discuss both the views and include your own opinion.

Recently there are more gas stations being built as opposed to diesel ones in rural areas. What are the advantages and disadvantages of this trend?

Many parents (mostly women) decide to stay home and take care of the family members instead of going out for work. Some people suggest that they should be paid by the government for doing that. Do you agree or disagree? Give reasons for your answer and include examples from your own experience.

Different cultures are mixing today and the world is becoming a global village. Is it a positive or a negative development? Give your own opinion and examples.

Nowadays people's life is changing rapidly and, as a result, family relationships are affected. Do the advantages of this outweigh the disadvantages? Give your opinion and examples from your own experience.

Measures have been put in place to improve road safety by reducing the speed limits. Some people believe there are better alternatives. Discuss both views and give your own opinion.

Some people think that the range of technology available to people is increasing the gap between the rich and the poor. Others think it has an opposite effect. Discuss both views and give your opinion.

Some of the methods used in advertising are unethical and unacceptable in today's society. To what extent do you agree or disagree with this statement?

People nowadays are not as fit and active as they were in the past. What are the reasons for this? What measures can be taken for this

Band 9 Answer Samples

In some countries, the average weight of people is increasing and their level of health and fitness is decreasing. What do you think are the causes of these problems and what measures could be taken to solve them? Give reasons for your answer and include any relevant examples from your own knowledge or experience.

You should write at least **250** words.

Sample Answer 1:

In many countries, the number of people who became overweight has increased and their health condition and fitness level are declining. This essay will discuss some of the reasons why these problems have arisen and some of the steps that can be taken to address them.

For a number of reasons, the average bodyweight of people in several countries is rising these days, and they have problems with the physical condition as well. Firstly, a lot of people prefer to consume in fast food outlets nowadays. It is undeniable that most of the fast food restaurants serve foods that contain fat and sugar, and as a result, those who frequently consume the food get overweight. Secondly, it is a fact business competition is getting tougher due to the globalisation, and people have to work for longer hours. They have to wake up very early in the morning to go to their workplace and arrive home late at night; therefore they have no time in doing some exercises. Consequently, many of these people have some serious health problems, such as obesity and diabetics.

There are several things that people can do to resolve the problems. One of them is that people should be more selective in choosing their diets. People should avoid in consuming fast food since they contain a lot of high cholesterol ingredients which are dangerous for their health. They should consume more of the healthier ingredients such as wheat, oat, vegetable or fruit rather than consuming fried chicken or hamburger. The other thing is that people should do more physical exercises and burn more calories in their life. One of the ways is by changing their mode of transportations. For example, they could change the way they commute from driving a car to riding a bicycle. It is not just making the body healthier, but bike riding also reduces air pollution as well.

In conclusion, it is true that many people are having problems with bodyweight and health conditions these days. The problems are mostly caused by the unhealthy lifestyles and there are several things that people could do to fix the problems. They should be more selective in choosing their diets and they should have more exercises in their life.

[by - Darwin Lesmana]

Essay Type: **Causes and Solutions.**

The main question of this IELTS Essay:

A. Why people's weight is increasing and their health condition and fitness are decreasing in many countries?

B. What measures could be taken to solve these problems?

Causes: Why people's weight is increasing and their health condition and fitness are decreasing in many countries?

- The popularity of eating high-calorie fast foods across the world.
- People have become less active than before due to changing of lifestyle (Using more private vehicles, using machines to do their tasks, or sitting in front of the computer and TV).
- The role of food advertisement in the media, which has tremendously increased the rate of obesity among children.
- Producing more variety of high caloric food products by food companies compared to the past.
- Shortage of health budget in some developing countries due to overpopulation and obese patients are less monitored by doctors.
- Trusting to other commercial methods for weight losing. People have less monitoring on their weight because they think there are better methods than sports to lose their weights.
- The role video games and computer games on children's inactivity.
- People's busy lifestyle forced them to depend on fast foods rather than cooking meals at home.
- Parents' carelessness often causes obesity among children.
- Ready to eat foods like chips, cheese and packet foods do more damage to our digestion system.
- The GM (Genetically Modified) foods contain high fats and we are consuming these GM foods every day.
- People's diet habit often makes them eat a large amount of food at a time rather than eating it in instalments.
- Lack of awareness, sedentary lifestyle and lack of exercise.
- People's choices of tasty but unhealthy foods lead them to gain weight.

Solutions: What measures could be taken to solve these problems?

- A healthy diet could be the best solution to tackle the obesity and health related issues.
- Restricted legislations on TV food advertisements by governments.
- School authorities must encourage young to do more daily exercise.
- Timely consumption of meals and ensuring that they are full of nutrition's is the key factor in living a healthy lifestyle.

- Considering more substantial health budget for obesity and its side effects.
- Avoiding GM foods and eating more fresh and organic vegetables and fruits.
- Popularising bicycle as a more leading method of transportation in many cities.
- Increasing the number of sports facilities.
- Increasing sports facilities in schools and encouraging children to do exercise more.
- Commercial methods for losing must be banned by health authorities.
- Increasing the awareness of people about the heinous effects of obesity.
- Parents should be more attentive to their children's health.
- Arranging sports and exercise facilities at the workplaces.
- People must be trained by the local council about how much is obesity dangerous for their health.
- Unhealthy foods must be banned from schools.
- Drinking a lot of water every day and avoiding alcohol totally.
- Avoiding fast food and drinks that contain high fat and sugar.
- Having more trained teachers who know more about children's diet.
- A healthy lifestyle, balance diet, exercise, outdoor activities can reduce this problem to a great extent.
- Monitoring packet foods and fast food items and their ingredients by the food authority are required to control the quantity of fats and sugars these items contain.
- Walking, making face-to-face communication and using the bicycle whenever possible.

Sample Answer 2:

Nowadays, with the advancement of technology and changes in lifestyles, new and eccentric problems have arisen in the society. Obesity which was a rare sight in the past has become more of a common sight. As most of the developed countries around the world are now facing this issue, the World Health Organization has decided to enlist obesity as a medical condition.

Two reasons could be listed down as the main cause for Obesity: firstly, the excessive consumption of fatty food, also known as junk food. Living in a society where time is of utmost importance, people tend to eat foods which are easy and quick to consume. It is this unhealthy diet that consists mostly of fatty food, which is the prime cause of obesity. Secondly, the busy lifestyle which the current society lives in is another reason for this health condition. People travelling in vehicles, using escalators, avoiding every task which needs physical exertion has made them lazy and unhealthy.

A healthy diet is the best remedy for obesity. Timely consumption of meals and ensuring that they are full of nutrition's is the key factor in living a healthy lifestyle. Fresh fruits and home grown vegetables provide those necessary nutrition's required. In addition to this, exercise and sports help in burning excessive fat and help reducing weight.

In conclusion, it is beyond a doubt that obesity is a rapidly growing health concern nowadays. It is time for us live a healthy life for the sake of our next generation. A well-planned diet and plenty of exercises would give birth to a generation that is fit, healthy and above all happy.

[by - **Inam Imthiyaz**]

Sample Answer 3:

According to a study, the average weight of people is increasing in few countries, which is, in turn, reducing their stamina and immunity levels. Overweight is always a problem and overweight causes numerous diseases and reduces the fitness.

A healthy human body on an average needs 2000 calories per day. Anymore added calories can cause more harm than good. There are few causes which contribute to this problem. Firstly, the type of foods intake and more advancement in technology is resulting in processed food, which is high in sugar and salt levels. Ready to eat foods like chips, cheese would cause more damage to our digestion system. Secondly, in few countries like India, people eat food at once in large amount instead of eating it in instalments. This habit would result in digestion problems.

Thirdly, proper intake of water is another important factor that many people simply ignore. It is said that 3 litres of water per day can avoid any digestion problems. Lastly, lack of exercise: many people, especially in corporate cultures, spend most of their time in front of the desk. Due to these highly pressurised jobs, they find very less time to take walk for at least 10 minutes. As a result of these reasons, a healthy person becomes obese.

These causes can be counter measured by following a proper diet which includes all food categories like fruits, vegetables, meats instead of readymade food, hydrating our body across the whole day. And finally, walking should be induced in our daily routine for at least 30 minutes. It is said that "Prevention is better than cure ".Though we have time constraints with our busy schedules we have to balance between our routine and health.

[by **Anila Poch**]

Sample Answer 4:

Weight-related issues have been on the rise in certain countries resulting in fitness levels moving towards a downward trail. The cause of the issue and preventive measures that can be taken is addressed in this article.

The major causes of weight gain in human beings can be attributed to dietary habits and a sedentary lifestyle. The human body is primarily designed to do physical work to digest the food consumed. Inadequate physical exercise leads to fat getting deposited mostly around the stomach and waist areas. Modern food habits are also a major contributor to weight gain. Excess consumption of processed and fatty foods can result in an obese and disease-prone body. Technological development has produced machines that perform work which was once done entirely by humans. This has caused human beings to become lazy and rely on machines even for the smallest possible physical work.

Research has shown that citizens of countries whose government emphasis on physical activities (sports) in schools and universities lead a disease-free life. While the issue of weight gain is a serious one, there are a number of simple measures that can be taken to address it. A personal acquaintance of mine had major issues with obesity. Regulated food habits, combined with a disciplined lifestyle and plenty of physical exercises worked wonders for him. Within a matter of months, he became leaner, fitter and extremely cheerful. Governments should create health-awareness programs that throw light on the ill-effects of weight gain and the numerous benefits of maintaining good health. Public swimming pools, jogging grounds should be provided and citizens must avail them at every opportunity.

As the old adage goes "A sound mind resides in a sound body". It is the responsibility of each individual to maintain proper body weight and set an example to their near and dear ones to achieve the goal of a disease-free society.

[by **Kalyan**]

Sample Answer 5:

In recent years, there is an increasing trend of obesity among individuals. Overweight is creating several health and fitness related problems. Allow me to analyse the reasons for this issue and possible remedial action. The essay will discuss the possible cause, lack of exercise and the available solution options.

Lack of physical exercise attributes as the prime reason for overweight. For example, with the increasing desk jobs and personal comfort, people end up working eight hours a day in front of a computer and travel in the comfort of their personal car. Once they reach home, they spend the majority of the time in front of the television. This lifestyle reduces the amount of physical activity of a person and contributes to their weight gain. Thus, lack of exercise impacts the amount of weight a person gains in a negative way. Increasing popularity of fast food is another major reason for the overweight. People's choices of tasty but unhealthy foods lead them to gain weight and finally, this food habit creates the obesity problem.

Required steps have to be taken to ensure that weights of individuals are in the right ratio per the body mass index; an index used to calculate the appropriate weight for height and weight. Involving in sports related activities and exercise could create wonderful benefits for the body. For instance, football and volleyball are the games that can be played to keep a person fit. Running can also increase the physical stamina of a person. By exercising sports related activities and cross-training activities body weight can be maintained at the correct level. Therefore, improving the duration of physical activities will reduce the overweight gained.

To conclude, reduction in the physical activities contributes to the majority of the individual's weight and health related problems. Indulging in sports activity or joining a cross-training gym is the suggested remedial action to overcome the problem. In coming years I think everyone should spend times to take care of their health by indulging in physical activities.

[by **Rajaganapathy**]

Sample Answer 6:

Obesity is progressing worldwide and the number of overweight population is increasing in many countries. Moreover, physical fitness and health status is deteriorating. I believed that environment, inactive lifestyle and food industry are just some of the causes leading people to overweight. These problems can be resolved but thoughtful lifestyle and food habit should be changed.

Fast food places are everywhere. People often buy foods to save money and time from those fast food shops. However, fast foods have a lack of nutrients and contain fats and sugars in a high amount which can cause health problems later on. Moreover, physical inactivity and laziness linked to the advancement of technology encourage obesity. For example, most individuals prefer to stay at home and they either work on their computers or play with their gadgets rather than going outside for a walk or doing outdoor activities. Another reason is the invention of cars and motorcycles which are convenient for travellers but a passive way of transportation thus resulting in decreasing of physical fitness. In addition, the food industry has a great impact on society. For an instance, food advertisements sometimes mislead the consumers by giving false information and sway people to buy high caloric foods.

The solution should start within individual's efforts and supports from the government. Each and every one of us is responsible for looking after ourselves. Engaging in physical activities, providing our body with healthy & nutritious diets, avoiding vices can lead toward life betterment. The other solution would be a support coming from the government such as promoting physical activity programs in the community. An example of this is to have a free outdoor exercises or dance at the park. This can be an effective way to persuade people to be physically active while enjoying others company. Also, implementing of proper food education at school and having a healthy set of meals at the canteen help the students to receive the nutrients they need.

To conclude, there are several factors that can affect the rising number of obesity population and decline of physical fitness and level of health. These can be solved with collaboration between government programs and people's efforts towards a healthy society.

[by - **Hera Andrea Panerio**]

Sample Answer 7:

Healthiness plays a vital role in human lives. It is true that people's average weight is growing in many nations due to several factors that degrade their strength. There are various reasons why individual's average weight is being increased, but they could certainly take steps to address this issue.

Firstly, the variety of food is different in each country that could increase people's weight, and the fitness standard reduces drastically. For instance, many western countries people used to have foods in such as pizza and burger which leads to obesity and surge in their weight that causes their health level. Moreover, people used to skip their breakfast to keep them fit because of which their weight gets increased after some point of time. The food with proper quality, less cholesterol would control their weight and keep them fit that lead to healthy life in near future. In addition, people should have their meals in proper timing to avoid any health related issues.

Secondly, the lack of exercise is one of the reasons for human's weight control. Most of the people are lazy to do any daily exercises that affect their health directly. For example, people intend to use bus or train to travel for even small distance and also people are using lifts instead of steps for small distance walk in their work premises as well. As a result, human average weight is increasing drastically now a day in many countries. As a corrective measure, people should walk daily at least a couple of kilometres where it is possible and also do basic exercise to keep them fit and that would improve the health standard.

In conclusion, various measures can be taken to tackle the problems that are certain to average weight increase to peoples in many nations to maintain their health standard at a high level.

[by - **Manickam**]

Sample Answer 8:

Over the last ten years, there are increasing numbers of overweight people around the world and at the same time, unfortunately, people do less exercise and have more health problems. Indeed, it is not a surprise that the number of fast food restaurants has increased and people have started to be busy and some of them lazy. This essay will discuss two reasons why this has occurred and examine the consequences of this worrying trend.

The main cause of the problem of obesity is the prolific increase in the number of fast food restaurants. For example, MacDonald's, Hungry Jack's, Pizza Hut. The advertisement of these restaurants focused on children to attract their attention, thus, increasing the number of customers amongst children. However, not only this, hard working people do not have time to prepare a healthy food at home, instead, they buy processed food such as sausages and meatballs in the closest stores. Also, in the rapidly developing society, there is a need to work harder and spend more hours at the workplace.

The measures of this problem have been and will continue to be taken. Firstly, in the TV famous people need to talk more about obesity as a major problem around the world that leads to serious health consequences such as diabetes. Secondly, it is important to promote a healthy lifestyle and life-work balance, which already have been done and will continue to be done. Not only this, great development was introduced to the market, which helps to measure how many steps did a person do during the day. If people start to use it, this will encourage them to do more necessary exercise during the day.

To sum up, it is evident that there are several causes of obesity and a variety of negative effects. Society must ensure steps are taken to prevent this problem from deteriorating further.

[by - Natalia Svetlova]

Sample Answer 9:

Throughout history, humans faced a wide range of illnesses. Some of the ailments rely on region and country but some parts of illnesses depend on culture. Yet there are some health issues which are global, for example, obesity which is one of the mankind's malicious problems, regardless of the race and region. In addition, during recent years, overweight and obesity increased so much that people and government should consider this issue very seriously.

21st century and technology advancement of it brought us computers, televisions, mobile phones, cars, lifts etc. Those gadgets, tools and devices prevent people from moving and compelling them to sit. So it is clear that one origin of obesity is overusing of computers, cars and televisions. Moreover, people don't join sports clubs and don't care with regard to doing regular exercise and this leads to unhealthy human generation. Furthermore, the fast food industry has the biggest impact on our health. Unhealthy foods with high fat, low nutrition, less use of vegetables, conservative items in foods are just some part of dark sides of this industry and obviously, this industry is the greatest factor in this obesity and health problem matters.

Handling this problem requires the support of government and they should be worried regarding the health issues of people. In some European countries, government obliged people to do exercise at least 5 hours per week. In addition, America legislates a rule that in line with it each person must eat at least 7 house maid meals per week. People need to be aware of their health. A healthy lifestyle, balance diet, exercise, outdoor activities can reduce this problem to a great extent.

To sum up, it can be argued that there are industries which invite us to taste their cheap, delicious and also unhealthy food. However, governments restricted those industries but people should care about their health personally and teach their children with regard to this matter.

Sample Answer 10:

The present generation is steering towards an unhealthy lifestyle resulting in obesity. This is at an alarming rate in some countries and is spreading wider across the globe. While overweight poses a threat to health and fitness of the current generation, also passing the risk to the future generation as well. There are several factors for this issue and this essay will shed light on a couple of them with possible solutions.

Firstly, the technological advancement is to be blamed. The growing number of computer-based jobs have restricted employees to minimal physical activities, and the introduction of intra-office messaging has further reduced the need for people to move around. For instance, in most software companies, the culture of messaging to colleagues who are in the adjacent cubicles is increasing. The solutions will be to encourage the employees to have intermittent breaks with simple stretching exercises. Also, they could be encouraged to have more face-to-face communication, thereby, not just achieving a physical activity, but also workplace integration.

Another important factor is the growing fast food consumption. Marketed as quick-to-prepare, these processed foods have several ingredients, which possibly remain the major reason for obesity. For example, fast food chain like KFC and Mc Donald's are known to serve burger and chicken with a greater amount of calories, which may not be required for a single meal. The solution is with the government to educate people about the health hazards so that people learn to avoid processed food. Also, the government could enforce the companies to manufacture much healthier food thereby contributing to a healthier society.

To conclude, both the people and government should work together to address the issue on the obesity. It will not just reduce their weight, but also an increased life with a greater health and fitness.

[by - **Balaji Mani**]

Sample Answer 11:

There are several reasons that cause the health's breadth and fitness decreased whereas people's average weight increased. Honestly, this is a serious problem for health. Nonetheless, it can be solved by some thoughtful and prudent attempts.

First of all, it is related to the job. Some people, who work in the office, always have a long time in the office since early morning until night for six days and probably they just have a day to take rest. Because of that, they think that there is no rest time, so the amount of food consumption always raises but the sports programs like fitness is never done by them. When they have a leisure time, of course, they just sleep. In addition, one of the reasons of their weight is never doing sports although they are workers.

Furthermore, the activities of jobless, some people who are spending their time in their houses, just eat and sleep without doing any physical exercises like jogging. These activities enforce them to achieve a high weight and making the obesity problem. Fast food outlets and people's dependency on them is another reason for obesity. To solve this problem, individuals need to put more concern on their own health. They should take a balanced diet, lead a healthy life, do some exercises daily and take advice from physicians. The government can take many initiatives like adding more sports facilities in the community; strictly control the junk food outlets, and encourage people to walk or use bicycles on the roads.

In conclusion, while they are workers or jobless they must be able to manage their time to balance the time for work, rest and doing sports like jogging. Although it is a simple sport but has a big impact on health. By doing this, the average of weight and health will balance.

[by - **Melanesia Boseren**]

Sample Answer 12:

Weight and health of a person are inter-related aspects. Nowadays, it seems that obesity has become a significant concern in some countries, as a result people there are getting relatively unhealthy than before. In this essay, the factors relating to over-weight and the ways to tackle them would be discussed.

There seem to be various reasons on why people become a victim of obesity. Firstly, the popularity of public and private vehicles have, to a large extent, discouraged people from walking to their works, shopping places etc. Secondly, there are few people who are regularly involved in some forms of exercises to burn their calories. Furthermore, the increasing trend of intake of junk foods like noodles, chips and cafeteria products as burgers, pizzas etc. have significantly contributed to dumping calories in people. For example, a guy from my neighbourhood does not go to the gym and takes a large amount of high-calorie fast foods. As a result, his weight is 74 kg while he is only 20 years old.

Modifications in sedentary lifestyles and proper diet could certainly address the problem to a large extent. To be more specific, consumption of calorie should be done according to the body requirements, by calculating the age, height-weight ratio. Diet should be balanced, inclusive of fats, carbohydrates, vitamins and minerals in required quantities rather than just oily and spicy. Additionally, exercises are also inevitable factors for a healthy body and it should be encouraged among all age groups. One should be motivated to give up sedentary habits and lead a more active life by walking, running, jogging, going to the gym etc.

Therefore, I would like to conclude that inappropriate food habits and non-active lifestyles are the contributors to obesity which can only be dealt with careful meal planning and calorie burning activities.

[by - **Sajana Koirala**]

Sample Answer 13:

It is believed that people in some countries are gaining more weight and their health and fitness are deteriorating. In my opinion, unhealthy lifestyle and sedentary nature of work are the main reasons for these health issues.

Firstly, people are becoming lazy and they want everything without making any effort. People who are unlikely to do exercise regularly are more prone to gain more weight. In addition, due to development in modern technology, most of the works are done through machines at home. For example, people use washing machines to do their laundry which does not require any physical effort. Furthermore, people consume fast foods increasingly that are rich in calorie.

Secondly, many people in developed countries spend most of their tie in front of computers, sitting in the chair whole day. Moreover, people do not walk to their office, even if it is at walking distance. They do not want to use the staircase, but elevator and lift are being used in every building and office. This is certainly contributing considerably to add unnecessary body weight.

Finally, to tackle these serious health issues, simple but regular physical exercise can be helpful. In addition to exercise, people need to reduce intake of high-calorie food on a daily basis. Taking a short walk to purchase vegetables, daily, instead of driving a car or commuting to office by foot, if it is near, can improve health to some extent.

In conclusion, to reduce these pressing health issues of increasing unnecessary body weight, people should do physical exercise regularly and avoid consuming too much fat.

Sample Answer 14:

The overweight of people is a global issue as the number of obese people is increasing in many countries. At the same time, the quality of their health and fitness are declining. Some individuals assume that these matters are occurred because of over-consumption of fast foods, sedentary lifestyle and lack of consciousness. In spite of the horrible effects of this lifestyle, people can minimize those trends by eating some organic vegetables and fruits frequently and doing exercise regularly.

To begin with, fast foods are the major cause of overweight. Every person who loves consuming these meals has a tendency to obtain inappropriate weight, particularly, obesities. In fact, junk foods contain less nutrition and more fat. This circumstance may come from ingredients which are used to produce the foods. Fast foods, in most of the cases, contain ingredients which are harmful to our body and cause rapid weight gain.

Secondly, people nowadays live a sedentary lifestyle and rely on technology to do their tasks. They even rely on ready-made foods to avoid cooking at home. Reliance on the computer and the internet has decreased their outdoor activities and very few people these days participate in sports and exercises. As a result, their health condition is decreasing as well as weight is increasing.

Finally, the lack of consciousness among people is another reason for this to happen. Apart from teens and children most of us know the harmful side effects of fast food intake and not doing exercises. Yet, we choose to live a life that we know would be harmful to us.

However, the preceding issue can be deterred by few steps. Firstly, people should get used to purchasing organic vegetables and fruits which do not contain chemicals. Although the prices of these organic foods are not cheap as non-organic one, benefits are indispensable to support our healthy. Secondly, it is often stated that to keep your body in good condition requires exercises daily basis. Doing sport can be adequate help to obtain ideal weight. For instance, going to the gym every week and walking in the evening can keep our body from being sick. We need to avoid fast foods as much as possible and put more effort on staying healthy by getting involved in physical exercises. The government can build more sports centers and gyms to encourage people to take part in exercises and reducing pollution would be another effective measure that should be ensured from the government's end.

In brief, people may choose to eat fast foods; however, this behavior can cause serious health issues. It would be better if people seek more information about the foods and doing sport to decrease the disadvantages of fast foods.

Grammar

Passive Forms

Use Past Simple Passive when we don't know who did something.

The bendable straw was made in the 1930s somewhere in the United States.

Passive forms are used in news reporting, scientific writing and other kinds of writing where we are more interested in events and processes than in the person doing the action.

A factory was set alight during the weekend and two million pounds' worth of damage was caused.

When the situation is in the present and the sentence needs to be impersonal - the passive form of the verb plus the infinitive:

The President is believed to be in contact with the Russians.

He is said to have poisoned his opponents in order to gain power.

Same situation in the past - passive plus the past infinitive:

Politicians in Burkina Faso are said to use underhand tactics, such as poisoning, against their opponents in order to gain power.

Second, third, and mixed conditionals

The **second** conditional is used to talk about unlikely or imaginary states or events in the present or future (form = **if** + **past simple/continuous** + **would/could/should/might**).

They would leave their jobs tomorrow and travel the world if they had the money.

The **third** conditional is used to talk about imaginary states or events in the past (form = **if** + **past perfect** + **would/ could/should/might** + **have** + **past participle**).

If they had studied other cultures at school, they might have been more confident about travelling.

If my parents had never met, I wouldn't be here now!

MIXED Conditional: A **third** conditional **cause** is sometimes linked to a **second** conditional **result** to show the **imaginary present result of an imaginary past event or situation.**

If pollution had been brought under control earlier, activists such as Greta Thunberg would not have appeared.

MIXED   Conditional: A **second** conditional **cause** is
sometimes   linked   to   a **third** conditional **result** to
show **how an ongoing situation produced an effect
in the past.**

*If he knew about computers, he
would have applied for that IT
job.*
*If the new workers were more
proficient with technology, they
would have (undoubtedly)
applied for positions in the IT
department.*

Wish/Would Rather

Talking about the past – things you regret
doing/not doing: **wish / if only + past perfect**

*Many parents wish they had not been
so strict with their children when they
were very young.*

Talking about the present – things that haven't
come true now and things that might come true
in the future: **wish / if only + past simple**

*They wish they were lying on a beach
somewhere instead of being here.*

Both **were** and **was** are   acceptable   but **were** is
more **formal**.

*Numerous IT students wish they were
working for companies instead of
constantly preparing for exams.*

*He wishes his daughter would make
smarter decisions.*

Talking about irritating habits – things which are
annoying you: **wish / if only + would**

*The electorate of Burundi wish their
elected officials would make wiser
decisions.*

*She'd rather we had gone to an Italian
restaurant.*

Would rather + past perfect is used to talk
about wishes in the past.

*The government of London would
rather implement face recognition
technology than increase the amount of
Police on the streets.*

Would rather + infinitive without to is used to
talk generally about wishes in the present and
future.

*The government would rather not give
out too many benefits to young people.*

Modals for speculation and deduction

could, might, may used to speculate about
something the speaker or writer is unsure

*It could be a possible reason for air
pollution, though the scientists are still*

about:

doubtful.

That possible new home we're looking at might in fact be Mars.

The answer to this situation may be to readvertise the job.

Banning fossil fuels completely cannot be one of the possible solutions for improving energy efficiency.

can't/cannot and couldn't/could not used to indicate certainty, in relation to impossible ideas and situations:

Banning fossil fuels completely, cannot (conceivably) be one of the possible solutions for improving energy efficiency.

could have, might have, may have are used to express uncertainty about something in the past.

The dinosaurs may have survived without the meteor impact that seriously altered weather patterns at the time.

must have is used to express near-certainty about something in the past.

It must have been bitterly disappointing for those citizens who had hoped for political change.

Advanced Collocations

have a significant impact on

fundamentally different

meet their targets

stimulate growth

a slight decrease/increase

achieve good marks

meet the requirements

stick to your diet

bombard sb with

have a natural talent for

formal education

reach agreement

public/peer pressure

major development

key advantage

have a thirst for adventure/ have a real sense of adventure

take up the challenge

score an own goal

draw up a schedule and stick to that schedule

careful consideration

a bold experiment

highly recommend

offer constructive criticism

pass new laws relating to

face severe weather conditions

absolutely essential/vital

vehicle emissions/carbon emissions

change our ways

changing weather patterns

harmful to the environment

keep my balance

reliable public transport

cost-cutting measures

extensive plans

a desirable place to live

the hectic pace of life

long-term investment

extend opportunity

the government is committed to its eradication

address the social issue

tackle the problem

offer a novel solution

dysfunctional families

Antisocial behavior

it is of great importance

jump to conclusions

allocate budget to

win a scholarship

engage in conversation

considerable success

change the subject

make a rash/empty promise

that's a tough question

got stuck in traffic

arduous journey

keep in shape

implement a plan

exercise control over

put their ideas into practice

strongly influences

create the atmosphere

a lasting impression on

reach an agreement

have an obligation to

irreversible climate change

alternative energy sources

long-term solutions

the risks to public health

damage the environment

high-quality urban living

financial crimes

to solve financial problems

commercial and recreational facilities

sth is on the increase

current economic climate

stimulates economic growth

curb inflation

drunk driving

offer a long-term solution

to be in crisis

underage drinking

take draconian measures

take up a lot of space/room

the strong economy
provide shelter
keep a balance between
a rich tradition of
deserve harsh punishment
part of the cultural heritage
long-standing tradition
technology is pushing back the frontiers of knowledge
switch channels
publish findings
build up your strength/resistance
gentle exercise
what is in fashion
be a fashion victim
heavy/dense traffic
traffic problems
a straight A student
to be in poor health
fight for his life
a substantial decrease/increase
go clubbing
express views about
the perfect venue
set objectives
collateral damage
carry out a survey/a study
recent research indicates that
first-hand knowledge
make a friend for life
healthy competition
child prodigy
provide an excellent service
notice a trace of sth
entirely agree
fundamentally disagree
reveal secrets
realize his ambition
make a success of sth
have respect or no respect for sb
mindless violence
betray trust
don't belittle their achievements
practical experience /skills
arouse my interest
mitigating factors

low- income families
poor sanitary conditions
unfit for
human habitation
to be vigilant about
work as a force for change

access my email
store music
maintain/enjoy good health
do plenty of exercise
do a lot of sport
watch what u eat
a course of medication
a serious medical condition
side effects
beneficial/adverse effect
a rare disease
untimely death
a special occasion
have a cold
crime rates
serve justice
escalate violence
seize power
bring stability
lift the sanctions on
fragile peace
close friends
long-term relationship
make a considerable contribution to

respect his wishes
rekindle memories of old days
highly praised
have a significant impact on
enjoy great success

the blame rests with

have a keen interest in
pursue my interests
have interpersonal skills
it is of paramount importance

in broad agreement

have unbounded enthusiasm

I have nothing but praise for sb

face the tough challenge

handle difficult situations

get the chance

well-qualified people

provide entertainment

win the battle against

conduct an investigation into

wonderful personal qualities

carry out a study

carry out research

face the facts

suffer the consequences

came across sth

weighty problems/matters

take responsibility for their actions

widely inaccurate

highly educated

highly recommended

strongly influence'

make a contribution to

make suggestions

make improvements

create a convivial atmosphere

create a good/bad impression on

choose your approach

generally speaking

needless to say

disseminate information

hold the view

am open to offers

fight for survival

take priority over

a significant number of /amount of

a daunting task

master new skills

take on more responsibility

realize their potentials

fluctuate widely

adapt to changing 'circumstances

I really think

break relation with

produce the desired effects

have boundless energy

personality traits

meet the challenges

have confidence in

have advanced skills

highly educated/valued man

develop a good relationship with sb

have an advanced knowledge of

have considerable experience of

her strong point

burning desire for

boost confidence

unacceptable behavior

a warm/friendly / sunny smile

have an abrasive manner

confined space

in the distant future

we are short of space

shape our lives

the basic principle

perform /complete a task

feasible alternatives

adopt a method

a simple rule

immense asset

take a step-by-step approach

the easy option

hinder progress

face a problem

adverse weather conditions

encounter difficulties

respond to the emergency

catastrophic results

a wide range of/choice of

there is room for improvement

implement some changes

make necessary changes

remain unchanged

dramatic shift

abandon the policy

the primary/root cause of sth

compelling reasons

it is common knowledge that

face the consequences of his actions

rough idea

a widespread belief

different things suit different tastes

strike the balance between

a yawning gap

a team effort/joint effort

radical/fundamental/dramatic changes in

to be doomed to failure

news travels fast

the simple reason

I am really looking forward to seeing u soon

frame the question differently

confront the issue directly

establish communication with people

international problems

have a strong sense of purpose

get the recognition you deserve

a contributing factor

a flurry of interest/excitement aroused

offer a glimmer of hope/light

fundamentally different/similar

a clear/subtle distinction between

bridge the gap between

make an strenuous/determined effort

provide a solution to the problem

devote energy to

have bright ideas

offer an explanation

strongly hope

discuss the issue

common problems

have a great sense of achievement

dreams come true

express my admiration for

Synonyms

English	**Synonyms for IELTS**
Amazing	Incredible, Fantastic, Fabulous, Astonishing, Extraordinary
Answer	Respond
Awful	Terrible, Abominable, Dreadful
Bad	Evil, Spoiled, Imperfect, Infamous, Dismal
Beautiful	Gorgeous, Ravishing, Dazzling, Exquisite, Stunning
Begin	Initiate, Commence, Inaugurate
Big	Huge, Enormous, Gigantic, Humongous, Substantial, Mammoth
Break	Rupture, Fracture, Shatter
Calm	Serene, Peace, Tranquil
Come	Approach, Arrive
Cool	Chilly, Frosty, Icy
Cut	Chop, Slash, Slit
Dangerous	Hazardous, Risky, Precarious
Decide	Determine, Settle
Definite	Certain, Positive, Obvious
Delicious	Savoury, Titbit, Delectable
Describe	Portray, Characterise
Destroy	Demolish, Slay, Ruin, Raze
Difference	Disagreement, Inequity, Dissimilarity
Dull	Boring, Uninteresting, Monotonous, Humdrum, Dreary
End	Terminate, Conclude, Cessation
Explain	Elaborate, Interpret
Fall	Drop, Descend, Topple
Famous	Well-known, Renowned, Eminent, Illustrious
Fast	Quick, Rapid, Hasty, Snappy, Swift
Fat	Stout, Corpulent, Chubby, Bulky
Funny	Amusing, Humorous, Droll, Hilarious

Get   Acquire, Obtain, Secure, Procure, Gather

Good   Excellent, Fine, Wonderful, Superior, Gracious, Superb, Splendid, Genuine, Sterling, Top-notch,

Great   Worthy, Distinguished, Grand, Considerable, Mighty

Happy   Pleased, Delighted, Elated, Joyful, Ecstatic, Jubilant, Jaunty

Hate   Despise, Loathe, Abhor, Abominate

Have   Possess, Own, Acquire,

Help   Aid, Assist, Support, Encourage, Relieve

Hide   Conceal, Cover, Mask, Veil

Idea   Thought, Concept, Notion

Important   Necessary, Vital, Critical, Indispensable, Valuable, Essential, Famous, Notable

Interesting   Fascinating, Engaging, Spirited, Intriguing, Gripping, Enthralling, Captivating

Little   Tiny, Diminutive, Exiguous, Dinky, Cramped

Look   Gaze, Glance, Peek, Glimpse, Stare, Leer

Love   Like, Admire, Fancy, Care for, Adore

Make   Create, Originate, Invent, Construct, Manufacture, Produce, Compose

Move   Plod, Creep, Crawl, Drag, Toddle, shuffle, Trot, Lumber, Meander

Neat   Orderly, Tidy, Trim, Natty, Smart, Elegant

New   Unique, Modern, Current, Recent

Old   Feeble, Ancient, Aged, Veteran, Mature, Primitive, Stale

Place   Draw, Map, Diagram, Procedure, Method, Blueprint

Show   Display, Exhibit, Indicate, Reveal, Demonstrate

Tell   Disclose, Reveal, Expose, Narrate, Inform, Divulge

Use   Employ, Utilise, Exhaust, Spend

Wrong   Incorrect, Inaccurate, Mistaken, Erroneous, Improper, Unsuitable

Useful Phrases

For many candidates IELTS essay is one big thing that hinders them from achieving a good score. If you are also one of those candidates who fear **IELTS Writing** essay and need some guidance, then you are at the right place.

Make use of these simple phrases or word-groups to make your essay more meaningful and attractive. But, take a note of it that the advice, suggestions or recommendations provided are for the purpose of practicing how to write well. You can make use of a few of them to begin your essay in your real IELTS exam too.

For introducing

You can introduce your essay in one of the following manners

- This essay will analyze (issue here)
- It is undeniable that the (issue here) is one of the most pressing issues in (country)
- It is an established fact that the (issue here)
- It is commonly believed in many of the countries that (issue here)

Phrases that can be used for the body paragraphs (Generally for the opinions / views)

If you are explaining an opposing thought, then it is better to begin with "However."

You can say as follows:

- However, it should be taken into consideration that (information here)
- However, it should be taken into account that the (information here).

Providing examples

In your essay, it will be important to support your views or opinions by providing some examples. These examples are often drawn from personal experiences. Based on the topic you will have to think of a good example that can support your opinions.

For instance, studies conducted recently by the (information here) show that (information here).

The problem can be better explained with the following example.

- A good example of this is that (information here)
- For instance, (information here)
- Such as (information here)
- The best example is (information here)
- There are many such cases that take place and that go unnoticed.
- It is fairly easy to understand the issues that are common
- I do not say that I agree with (information goes here)
- I strongly oppose / suggest / recommend that (information)
- Numerous studies conducted on this subject have led to the conclusion that (information).
- However, it can be concluded that (information)
- It is easy to comprehend that the (information here)
- Not all the people support this because (information)

Express your opinions using the following word-groups or phrases

- I believe that
- I think that
- I feel that
- Personally, I feel that
- As far as I am concerned
- In my views
- From my point of view / viewpoint

These are the common words that can be used when you have to combine two different sentences or thoughts

- Furthermore
- In addition to
- Likewise
- On top of that
- However
- But
- Nevertheless
- Additionally

Comparing two things

In your writing task in IELTS you will also have to be good at comparing things. There can be two or more than two things that you may have to compare. Make use of these common word groups or phrases to compare things in the right way.

- In contrast
- By comparison
- Comparing this with the other, it can be said that the latter is / the former is (information here)
- Meanwhile
- On the other hand
- However

Use the following word groups or phrases when you have to say that one thing will happen only after another thing happens

- On the condition that
- Provided that
- As long as
- Unless
- Supporting that
- Otherwise

Use these word-groups or phrases when you are introducing any reason

- As a result
- As a consequence
- Therefore
- Accordingly, that
- On that account
- For that reason

Vocabulary for IELTS Topic 1 : People

1. Self-esteem - belief in yourself

2. Stereotypical - having typical qualities

3. Fallible - able to make mistakes and be wrong

4. Sociable - friendly or seeking company

5. Tendency - recurring action or behavior

6. Gender - sex (male or female)

7. Lifetime - period of time you're alive

8. Empathize - understand someone's feelings

9. Hardwired - automatic behavior

10. Habitually -usually or repeatedly

Vocabulary for IELTS Topic 2 : Health & Fitness

1. Sedentary - sitting a lot or inactive

2. Psychological - mental

3. Beneficial - helpful or positive

4. Detrimental - harmful or negative

5. Intake - amount you take in

6. Eradicate - get rid of or eliminate or wipe out

7. Well-being - health and happiness

8. Severity - how serious something is

9. Preventive - deterrent

10. Additives - chemicals added to food

Vocabulary for IELTS Topic 3 : Science

1. Ascertain - make sure or establish

2. Breakthrough - important new discovery

3. Release - allow to escape (gas) or give off

4. Accumulate - collect over time, gather or build up

5. Absorb - take in or soak up (liquid or gas)

6. Synthetic - man made or artificial

7. Potential - ability or capability

8. Advances - progress or developments

9. Precise - exact or accurate

10. Quantify - count or measure

Vocabulary for IELTS Topic 4 : Community

1. Considerate - kind and helpful or thoughtful

2. Mainstream - common or average (ideas)

3. Civilization - culturally advance human society

4. Supportive - helpful and encouraging

5. Appropriate - suitable

6. Engage - join in or get involved

7. Voluntary - done willingly or without payment

8. Charitable - helping the poor or needy

9. Foster - help something grow (attitude or idea)

10. Multicultural - having many different cultures

Vocabulary for IELTS Topic 5 : Study

1. Specialize - concentrate on one subject

2. Profound - deep or intense (effect or feeling)

3. Cognitive - connected to thinking or mental

4. Curiosity - desire to know or find out /interest

5. Achievement - reaching a goal or success

6. Failure - lack of success or collapse

7. Determination - trying hard or not giving up

8. Miscalculation - bad judgement or calculation

9. Collaborate - work together with

10. Methodical - in a careful or ordered way

Vocabulary for IELTS Topic 6 : Advertising

1. Ignore - pay no attention

2. Endorse - recommend a product or brand

3. Guarantee - promise that S will happen

4. Gullible - easily tricked or too trusting

5. Prominent - noticeable / stand out

6. Pressure - forcefully persuade compel

7. Incorporate - use / include / contain

8. Entice - persuade by offering something / tempt

9. Bombard - attack continuously / pester

10. Inescapable - cannot be avoided/ unavoidable

Vocabulary for IELTS Topic 7 : Travel & Places

1. Caution - avoiding risks / wary

2. Wander - walk without aim / stroll / roam

3. Adventurous - willing to try new thing / daring

4. Spontaneous - act without planning / unplanned

5. Unspoiled - beautiful or undamaged (place)

6. Wilderness - land not used

7. Paradise - a perfect place

8. Leisurely - in a relaxed way / not rushed

9. foreign - strange or unfamiliar

10. Rival - be good as something else

01

Vocabulary for IELTS Topic 8 : Government

1. Guideline - official advice / rules

2. Consensus - general agreement / unity

3. Instill - put and idea or feeling in something mind

4. Taxpayer - person paying tax / ordinary citizens

5. Corrupt - dishonest / abusing their power

6. Expenditure - total amount a government spends

7. Resolve - firmly decide / undertake

8. Authority - legal power / right

9. Instability - lack of stability or uncertainty

10. Bureaucracy - admin system / official procedure

Vocabulary for IELTS Topic 9 : Animals

1. Survival - continuing to live or exit

2. Co-exist - live in the same time or place

3. Abandon - leave permanently / desert

4. Captivity - the state of being locked up

5. Cruelty - behavior that causes pain

6. Sanctuary - safe or protected place

7. Defense - reaction to attack / self-protection

8. Conservation - protecting them

9. Colony -

10. Creature - living thing

Vocabulary for IELTS Topic 10 : Space

1. Collide - crash into / strike

2. Universal - worldwide / existing everywhere

3. Misuse - bad usage of something

4. Boost - added power / increase

5. Hollow - empty inside

6. Prolonged - length / over a long time

7. Rotation - spinning / turning

8. Fragile - easily broken / delicate

9. Vertical - pointing going up

10. Transmit - send out (a signal)

Vocabulary for IELTS Topic 11 : Technology & Computer

1. Appliances - domestic machine

2. Creativity - imagination / ingenuity

3. Surpass - beat / outperform / do or be better than

4. Run-down - neglected / in a bad condition

5. Hardware - the physical parts of computer

6. upgrade - improve the quality

7. Innovative - inventive / a new use of something

8. Computerized - run or controller by computer

9. Devise - come up with / invent

10. Equipped - have (a tool) included or attached

Vocabulary for IELTS Topic 12 : Fashion

1. Ethical – morally right

2. Emerge – appear / arise

3. Disposable – intended to be thrown away

4. Second-hand – used / not new

5. Possessions – things you own / belongings

6. Donate – give money or goods to charity

7. Individual – what makes you different or unique

8. Impulse – sudden urge or desire

9. Manufacturer – company making goods / producer

10. Material – physical / related to possessions

Vocabulary for IELTS Topic 13 : City

1. Imbalance - inequality / lack of balance

2. Overwhelmed - unable to cope / strongly affected

3. Shortage - lack / not enough of

4. Affluent - rich / wealthy / prosperous

5. Deprived - poor / disadvantaged

6. Congested - having too much traffic

7. Sanitation - system to remove dirty water or waste

8. Homelessness - the issue of people having no home

9. Poverty - the condition of being poor

10. Amenities - facilities / conveniences

Vocabulary for IELTS Topic 14 : Environment

1. Urgent - pressing / needing quick attention

2. Pollutant - a substance that pollutes

3. Ecosystem - all living thing in an area

4. Vegetation - plants and tree in an area

5. Unprecedented - never seen before / unheard-of

6. Intervene - step in / become involved

7. Hazardous - dangerous to health or safety

8. Degrade - become spoiled or lower in quality

9. Safeguard - keep safe / protect

10. Deforestation - removal of tree / logging

Vocabulary for IELTS Topic 15 : Energy

1. Abundant - in large quantities / plentiful

2. Regulate - control something with rules

3. Scarce - not easy to find / rare

4. Supply - give or provide a supply

5. Unsustainable - using more than can be replaced

6. Squander - waste (money , supplies or opportunity)

7. Exploit - take advantage or make the most of

8. Bio-fuels - fuel made from a waste material (agricultural waste)

9. Achievable - realistic / attainable

10. Finite - limited / have end

Collocations

- **Verb + Noun**
- **Verb + Adverb**
- **Adjective + Noun**
- **Adverb + Adjective**
- **Noun + Noun**
- **Collocations with 'have' or 'take'**

Verb Noun collocations

a) It was his 21st birthday so he decided to **throw a party.**

b) The student **raised a question** about the topic in class.

c) The teacher **paid** him **a compliment** about his well written IELTS essays.

d) She was late for work so she **made an excuse** about the train being delayed.

e) The government is **giving priority** to the issue of air quality in cities.

f) I **made an appointment** to see the dentist.

g) The student **made an effort** to improve his essay writing.

Verb Adverb collocations

a) The customer **complained bitterly** about the terrible service.

b) The guests were **welcomed warmly** when they arrived at the party.

c) She **spoke loudly** over the phone because the signal wasn't very good.

d) He **smiled proudly** when he got his IELTS exam results.

e) He **apologised profusely** after bumping into the man and spilling his drink.

f) She is a very gentle person who **speaks softly**.

Adjective Noun collocations

a) The boy shows a **keen interest** in going to University and becoming a Doctor.
b) We had a **brief chat** about our travel plans next week.
c) There was **heavy snow** overnight, the roads were all blocked.
d) I was given **invaluable advice** from the teacher about doing the reading test.
e) He suggested going to the beach. It was a **fantastic idea** so we all decided to go.
f) There is a **strong possibility** that the climate will get warmer over the next two decades.

Adverb Adjective collocations

a) I was **utterly shocked** by his bad behaviour.
b) She is **totally satisfied** with her Band 8 score in IELTS
c) It is **incredibly stupid** to drink and drive.
d) The weather is **rather cold** for this time of year.
e) The new laws about internet privacy are **pretty worrying**.
f) I'm **extremely interested** in getting a Band 9 in IELTS.

Noun Noun collocations

a) There was **a ceasefire agreement** by the rebel groups.
b) I bought **a loaf of bread** and **a can of coke.**
c) He bought **a round of drinks** for his friends
d) He got **a round of applause** after his performance
e) They work in **the service industry**.
f) You need **a building permit** to build a house.

References:

IELTS   Podcast.Retirieved   from: https://www.ieltspodcast.com/sample-ielts-task-2-questions/

IELTS   Podcast.Retirieved   from: https://www.ieltspodcast.com/writing-task-2/ielts-grammar/

O'Dell, F., & McCarthy, M. (2017). English cllocation in use.

IELTS Advantage.Retirieved from: Ieltsadvantage.com

Printed by Books on Demand GmbH, Norderstedt / Germany